# A Note to Parents and Teachers

Kids can imagine, kids can laugh and kids can learn to read with this exciting new series of first readers. Each book in the Kids Can Read series has been especially written, illustrated and designed for beginning readers. Humorous, easy-to-read stories, appealing characters, and engaging illustrations make for books that kids will want to read over and over again.

To make selecting a book easy for kids, parents and teachers, the Kids Can Read series offers three levels based on different reading abilities:

### Level 1: Kids Can Start to Read

Short stories, simple sentences, easy vocabulary, lots of repetition and visual clues for kids just beginning to read.

### Level 2: Kids Can Read with Help

Longer stories, varied sentences, increased vocabulary, some repetition and visual clues for kids who have some reading skills, but may need a little help.

### Level 3: Kids Can Read Alone

Longer, more complex stories and sentences, more challenging vocabulary, language play, minimal repetition and visual clues for kids who are reading by themselves.

With the Kids Can Read series, kids can enter a new and exciting world of reading!

# Spooky Riddles

## Marilyn Helmer

## Eric Parker

Kids Can Press

Knock, knock.

*Who's there?*

Arthur.

*Arthur who?*

Arthur any monsters under the bed?

# What do witches put on their bagels?

Scream cheese

What do you get when you put three sloppy monsters in a room together?

A monster-ous mess!

How do you make a skeleton laugh?

Tickle her funny bone.

# When is the best time to meet King Kong?

When he isn't hungry!

# What's white and covered with red spots?

A ghost with measles

# What game do little goblins play on Halloween?

Hide and shriek

What time is it when Frankenstein sits on your bicycle?

Time to get a new bicycle

Who do vampires call when they are feeling sick?

Count Doc-ula

What should you say when you meet a two-headed monster?

Hello! Hello!

# What kind of stones do ghosts collect?

Tombstones

Knock, knock.

*Who's there?*

Ghoul.

*Ghoul who?*

Ghoul D. Locks and the Three Scares.

What did the vampire say when he saw the Count Dracula movie?

That was fang-tastic!

What does Godzilla eat for breakfast?

Bacon and legs

How did the ghoul sign his letters?

Yours ghoul-y

Why did the mother ghost dress her baby
in a blue sheet?

Because all the white ones were in the wash

# What cartoon do witches like best?

The Scare Bears

What happened to the mummy who ate too much candy?

He got a mummy ache.

What do you say to a naughty vampire?

You're a pain in the neck!

How do you unlock the door to a haunted house?

With a skeleton key

# Which monster wears the biggest shoes?

The one with the biggest feet, of course!

How do you make a witch itch?

Take away the *w*.

# Why did the dog dress up like a werewolf?

He wanted to go out for Howl-oween.

What does Dracula take when he has a bad cough?

Coffin drops

# Who grants wishes to unhappy goblins?

The scary godmother

# What was the witch's best subject in school?

Spell-ing

What is the difference between a monster and a peanut butter cookie?

It's harder to dunk a monster in a glass of milk.

What kind of dog do vampires keep as pets?

Blood-hounds

Where do you find ghosts at an amusement park?

Riding the roller-ghoster

# What does a witch wear on her left wrist?

A witch-watch, of course!

**For Samuel, who likes to tell riddles and write them, too. – M.H.**

Kids Can Read™ Kids Can Read is a trademark of Kids Can Press Ltd.

Text © 2003 Marilyn Helmer
Illustrations © 2003 Eric Parker

All rights reserved. No part of this publication may be reproduced, stored in a retrieval system or transmitted, in any form or by any means, without the prior written permission of Kids Can Press Ltd. or, in case of photocopying or other reprographic copying, a license from The Canadian Copyright Licensing Agency (Access Copyright). For an Access Copyright license, visit www.accesscopyright.ca or call toll free to 1-800-893-5777.

Kids Can Press acknowledges the financial support of the Ontario Arts Council, the Canada Council for the Arts and the Government of Canada, through the BPIDP, for our publishing activity.

Published in Canada by
Kids Can Press Ltd.
29 Birch Avenue
Toronto, ON M4V 1E2

Published in the U.S. by
Kids Can Press Ltd.
2250 Military Road
Tonawanda, NY 14150

www.kidscanpress.com

Edited by David MacDonald
Designed by Stacie Bowes and Marie Bartholomew
Printed and bound in Singapore

The hardcover edition of this book is smyth sewn casebound.
The paperback edition of this book is limp sewn with a drawn-on cover.

CM 03 0 9 8 7 6 5 4 3 2
CM PA 03 0 9 8 7 6 5 4 3 2 1

**National Library of Canada Cataloguing in Publication Data**

Helmer, Marilyn
Spooky riddles / Marilyn Helmer, Eric Parker.

(Kids can read)
ISBN 1-55337-447-9 (bound) ISBN 1-55337-413-4 (pbk.)

1. Riddles, Juvenile. I. Parker, Eric II. Title. III. Series:
Kids can read (Toronto, Ont.)

PN6371.5.H447 2003 jC818'.5402 C2002-904611-4

Kids Can Press is a Corus™ Entertainment company